A Visit to EGYPT

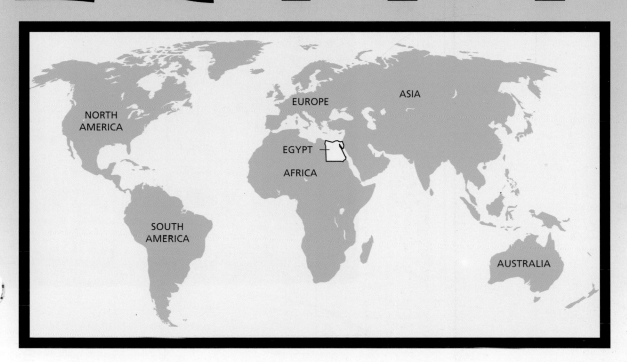

NORTH AMERICA

EUROPE

ASIA

EGYPT

AFRICA

SOUTH AMERICA

AUSTRALIA

Peter & Connie Roop

First published in Great Britain by Heinemann Library
Halley Court, Jordan Hill, Oxford OX2 8EJ
a division of Reed Educational and Professional Publishing Ltd.
Heinemann is a registered trademark of Reed Educational & Professional Publishing Limited.

OXFORD FLORENCE PRAGUE MADRID ATHENS
MELBOURNE AUCKLAND KUALA LUMPUR SINGAPORE TOKYO
IBADAN NAIROBI KAMPALA JOHANNESBURG GABORONE
PORTSMOUTH NH CHICAGO MEXICO CITY SAO PAULO

Designed by AMR
Illustrations by Art Construction
Colour Reproduction by Dot Gradations, U.K.
Printed in Hong Kong by Wing King Tong Co., Ltd.

02 01 00 99
10 9 8 7 6 5 4 3 2 1

ISBN 0 431 08317 7

This title is also available in a hardback edition (ISBN 0431 08308 8).

Roop, Peter
  A visit to Egypt
  1. Egypt – Social conditions – 1952 – Juvenile literature
  2. Egypt – Geography – Juvenile literature
  3. Egypt – Social life and customs – Juvenile literature
  I.Title II.Egypt
  962'.055

Acknowledgements
The Publishers would like to thank the following for permission to reproduce photographs:
J Allan Cash: p20; Ian Cook: p24; Robert Harding Picture Library: F J Jackson p19, E Simanor p25;
Hutchison Library: p22, S Errington p15, J Hart p14, Liba p28, Regent p8, L Taylor p23, B Wills p17;
Christine Osborne Pictures: pp 7, 9, 12, 13, 18; Peter Sanders: p29; Spectrum Colour Library: p26; Trip:
R Cracknell p6, E James pp 21, 27, P Mitchell p16, A Tovy p11; Zefa: p5, C Friere p10, Maroon p9.

Cover photograph reproduced with permission of Jorgen Schytte / Still Pictures.

Our thanks to Rob Alcraft for his comments in the preparation of this book.

Every effort has been made to contact holders of any material reproduced in this book.
Any omissions will be rectified in subsequent printings if notice is given to the Publisher.

Any words appearing in bold, **like this**, are explained in the Glossary.

Contents

Egypt

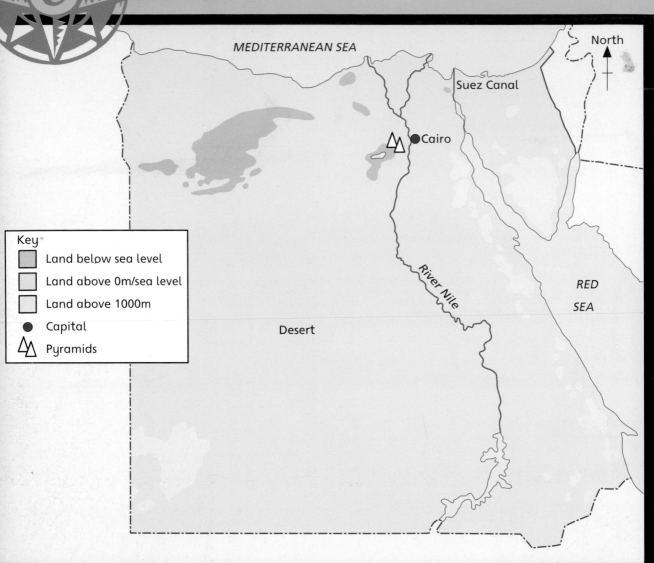

Key
- Land below sea level
- Land above 0m/sea level
- Land above 1000m
- ● Capital
- ⛰ Pyramids

MEDITERRANEAN SEA

Suez Canal

North

●Cairo

River Nile

RED SEA

Desert

Egypt is in the north-east corner of Africa.
It is shaped like a square.

Many people visit Egypt to see the **ancient** buildings. More than 2000 years ago the Egyptians built **temples**, the **pyramids** and the **Great Sphinx**.

Land

Egypt is a hot, dry country. **Desert** and mountains cover most of Egypt. The longest river in the world is in Egypt. It is called the River Nile.

Egyptians have lived along the River Nile for 5000 years. Today, nine out of every ten Egyptians still live near there.

Landmarks

Cairo is the **capital** of Egypt. It is also the largest city in Egypt and Africa. About 7 million people live in Cairo.

The Egyptians built the **pyramids** for their kings, called pharoahs. They put the body of the dead pharaoh inside the pyramid. They also put in beautiful clothes and jewellery.

Homes

The crowded Egyptian cities have old and new buildings. Most people live in small houses or flats.

In the country, homes are made of sun-dried bricks. The **Bedouin** people (above) live in the **desert**. They are always moving their tents to find food and water for their animals.

Food

Egyptians usually eat five small meals a day. They eat some food on the way to work or school. Food **stalls** sell snacks including rice, lamb and olives.

Egyptians eat ful everyday. Ful is a special mixture of spices, beans and tomatoes. Sweet **pastries** called havla and baklava are favourite snacks.

Clothes

Egyptians have many kinds of clothes. Some Egyptian men like to wear cotton trousers and a long shirt called a galabiyah.

Some Egyptian women wear a black dress, like a galabiyah. Many Egyptian women and children dress in bright colours.

Work

Many people are farmers in Egypt. They must water their **crops** often because Egypt is so dry. They grow vegetables, corn, sugar cane, cotton, rice, figs, grapes and dates.

Other people work with cotton, steel and oil **products**. These are important to Egypt because they can be sold to other countries.

Transport

Not many Egyptian people have cars. Most of them walk or travel by bus or train. They use boats called feluccas on the River Nile.

Egypt has a very important channel for ships. Big ships take a short cut through the Suez **Canal**. This saves them from sailing all the way around Africa.

Egypt's national language is Arabic. People also speak Greek, Italian, English and French.

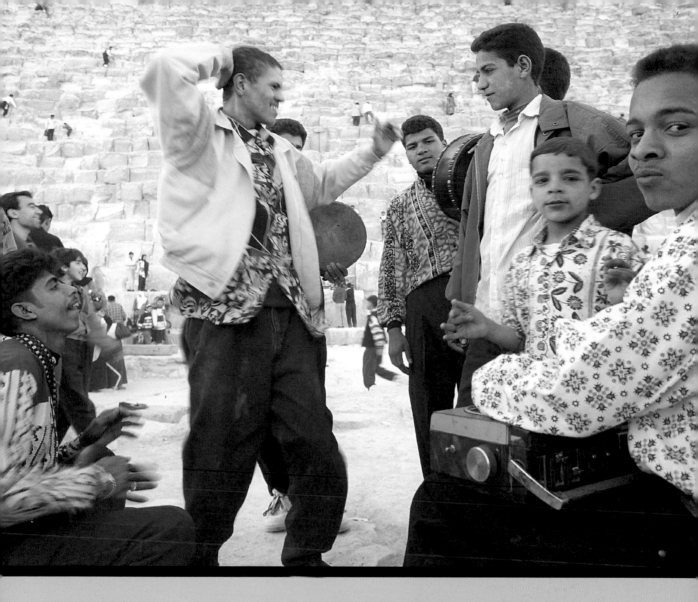

Egyptians speak 9 kinds of Arabic. Now Egyptians are creating one modern Arabic language. Soon they will all be able to understand each other.

School

All Egyptian children between the ages of 6 and 14 must go to school. Children learn maths, reading, science, music, French, English and art.

Egyptian children learn to read and write Arabic. Arabic has 28 letters. You read it from right to left.

Free time

Football (soccer) is a favourite Egyptian sport. People also play basketball, tennis, **squash** and volleyball. On hot days they swim in the River Nile to cool off.

Egyptians enjoy spending time at the souk. A souk is an outdoor market with lots of **stalls**. They shop and talk with friends and family.

Celebrations

In Egypt, families celebrate many special occasions together. Weddings are a time for dressing up in best clothes and enjoying good food and dancing.

Ramadan is the most important celebration for **Muslims**. People pray and **fast** for a month. Families get together to celebrate at the end of it.

The Arts

Films are a very popular art in Egypt. Many films are made in Cairo. Egyptians are also a musical people. They play their music on **lutes**, drums and tambourines.

Egyptians also enjoy reading. In 1988, an Egyptian writer named Nagub Mahfouz won the prize for the world's best writing.

Factfile

Name	The full name of Egypt is the Arab Republic of Egypt.
Capital	The **capital** city is Cairo.
Language	Most Egyptians speak Arabic.
Population	There are more than 56 million people living in Egypt.
Money	Instead of the dollar or the pound, the Egyptians have the Egyptian pound.
Religions	Most Egyptian people believe in **Islam** or Christianity.
Products	Egypt produces lots of oil, cotton, fruits and vegetables.

Words you can learn

ahlan wa sahlan	hello
ma'as salama	goodbye
ismi	My name is
shukran	thank you
aywa	yes
la'	no
waHid	one
itnein	two
talata	three

Glossary

ancient	from a long time ago
Bedouin	a group of people who live in tents in the desert
canal	river dug by people
capital	the city where the government is based
crops	the plants that farmers grow
desert	large areas of land that have little or no rain and very few plants or animals
fasting	not eating any or some kinds of food
Islam	the main religion of Egypt
lute	a musical instrument like the guitar, played by plucking the strings
Muslims	people who believe in the Islamic religion
pastries	food which are held in a crumbly dough called pastry
products	things which are grown, taken from the earth, made by hand or made in a factory
pyramids	the enormous stone buildings in the desert that have triangular sides
Great Sphinx	the huge stone sculpture built next to the pyramids, it has the body of a lion and the head of a human
squash	a game indoors, played with a racket and a hard ball
stalls	tables and shelves laid out with things for sale
temples	buildings used as places of worship

Index